SOUTH SAN FRANCISCO LIBRARY

W9-BOA-921

SSF

S.F. PUBLIC LIBRARY
WEST ORANGE AVENUE

APR   2003

DEMCO

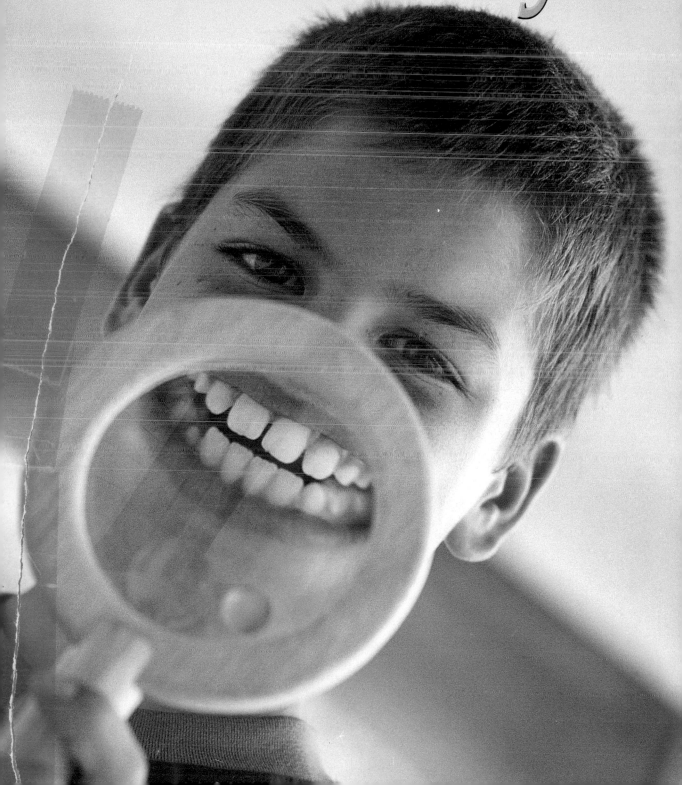

DK Eye Wonder
Human Body

S.S.F. PUBLIC LIBRARY
WEST ORANGE AVENUE

LONDON, NEW YORK, MUNICH,
MELBOURNE, and DELHI

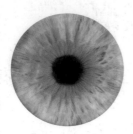

Written and edited by Caroline Bingham
Designed by Helen Melville

Managing editor Sue Leonard
Managing art editor Cathy Chesson
Category publisher Mary Ling
US editor Christine Heilman
Jacket design Chris Drew
Picture researcher Marie Osborn
Production Shivani Pandey
DTP Designer Almudena Díaz
Consultant Daniel Carter
Thanks to Penny Arlon for editorial assistance

First American Edition, 2003
03 04 05 10 9 8 7 6 5 4 3 2 1

Published in the United States by
DK Publishing, Inc
375 Hudson Street
New York, New York 10014

Copyright © 2003 Dorling Kindersley Limited

All rights reserved under International and Pan-American
Copyright Conventions. No part of this publication may be
reproduced, stored in a retrieval system, or transmitted in any form
or by any means, electronic, mechanical, photocopying, recording,
or otherwise, without the prior written permission of the copyright
owner. Published in Great Britain by Dorling Kindersley Limited.

Library of Congress Cataloguing-in-Publication Data
Bingham, Caroline, 1962-
Body / by Caroline Bingham ; consultant, Daniel Carter.
p. cm. -- (Eye wonder)
Includes index.
Summary: A brief introduction to the human body, including some
facts about sleep
ISBN 0-7894-9044-7
1. Body, Human--Juvenile literature. [1. Body, Human. 2. Sleep.] 1.
Carter, Daniel. II. Title. III. Series.
QM27 .B564 2003
306.4--dc21
2002009547
ISBN 0-7894-9044-7

Color reproduction by Colourscan, Singapore
Printed and bound in Italy by L.E.G.O.

See our product line at
www.dk.com

Contents

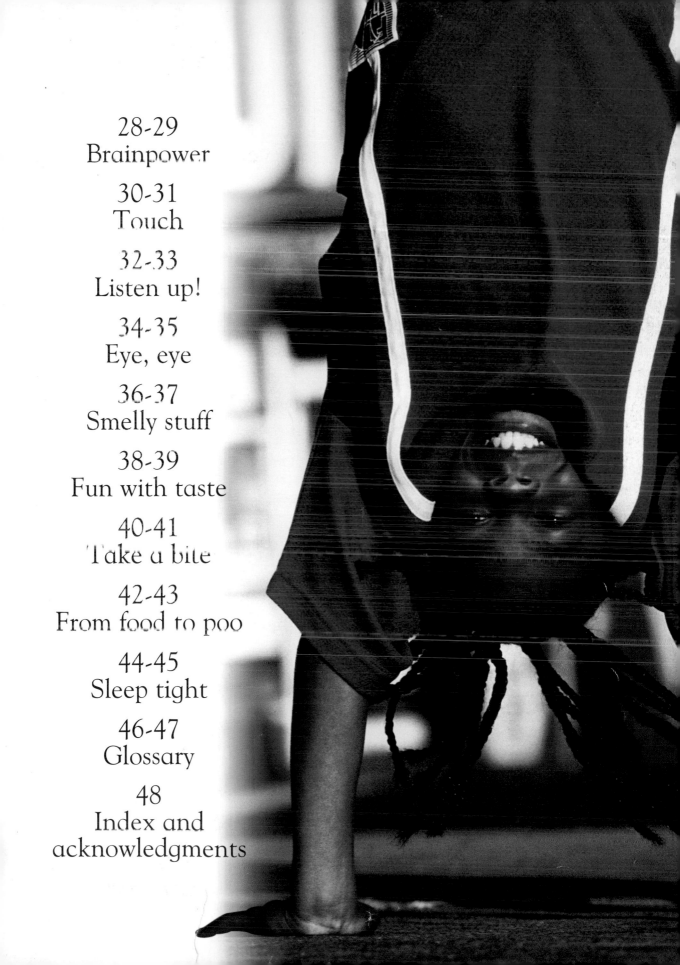

Everyone looks different...

Tall, short, plump, thin, blond, dark... Even though we have two eyes, a nose, two arms, and so on, we still all look so different that we can recognize each person we know without getting anyone confused.

Human beings are different in all sorts of ways. It is thought

Body facts

The average human body
contains enough iron to make
a nail 1 in (2.5 cm) long.

Brown or black skin has
more of a pigment called
melanin in it than white skin.

You inherit certain features
such as hair color or body
shape) from your parents.

What about twins?

Only identical twins
look alike, and that is
because they develop at
the same time, from one
egg that has split into
two. Identical twins are
always the same sex.

…at more than 6,500 languages are spoken throughout the world.

*There are slight differences
between the left- and right-
hand sides of your face.*

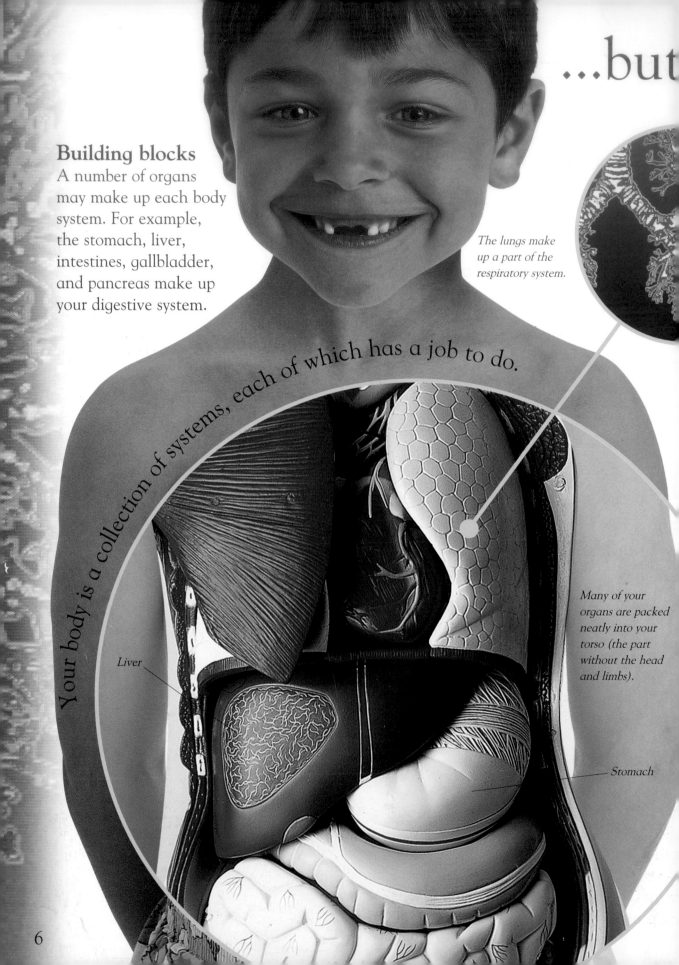

Building blocks

A number of organs may make up each body system. For example, the stomach, liver, intestines, gallbladder, and pancreas make up your digestive system.

The lungs make up a part of the respiratory system.

Your body is a collection of systems, each of which has a job to do.

Many of your organs are packed neatly into your torso (the part without the head and limbs).

Liver

Stomach

...but

...ve are all alike inside

All bodies are made up of organs. Skin is an organ. It is wrapped around a framework of bones and other organs such as the heart, the brain, and the lungs.

What does an organ do?

Organs work to keep you alive, and each does a different job. Organs work together to make up systems, such as the muscular system and the circulatory system.

It would take about 200 of your cells to cover a period.

A TALL STORY

The tallest man ever recorded, Robert Wadlow, grew to 8'11" (272 cm). He was born in the US in 1918, and died in 1940. He was known as the Gentle Giant. He grew so big because too much growth hormone was released into his body.

Your body has about 50,000 billion cells.

...lade of tissue

...rgans are made up ...f tissue, which is made ...f groups of similar cells. ...hese magnified cells ...e from the lungs.

Nucleus

Cell

...ifferent cells

...lls are different depending ...n the organ they are a part ...– skin cells, for example, are ...ferent from bone cells. Most cells ...ve a nucleus – the control center.

Babies and belly buttons

We all begin life inside our mother as a tiny egg. This develops after it is joined, or fertilized, by a sperm from the father. Most babies spend about 40 weeks growing in their mother's tummy.

Baby facts

- At just eight weeks, the fetus can be recognized as human – although it is shorter than your little finger.

- Fingernails begin to form when the fetus is about ten weeks old.

- A fetus can get hiccups.

A race to the eg

Millions of sperm swi toward the mother's egg fertilize it, though only abo one hundred get near it. Ju one sperm fertilizes

Legs here, arms there...

After the egg has been fertilized, it begins to divide, becoming a ball of cells. It is full of instructions for what the baby will look like.

They can hear you!

A baby can hear noises from around its mother's tummy – it can hear you talking or laughing, and it will recognize your voice.

The fetus is protected in a sac of fluid.

The cord that attaches a baby to its mother is called the umbilical cord.

How does it breathe?

The fetus cannot eat or breathe until birth, so it gets food and oxygen from its mother through a special cord. At birth this cord is cut, and shrivels away to leave the belly button.

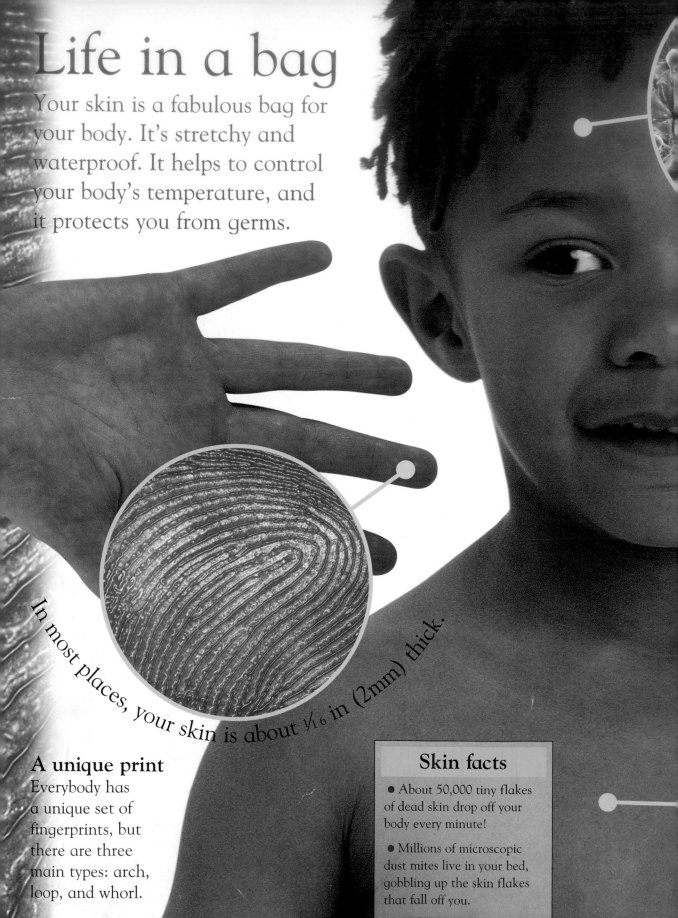

Life in a bag

Your skin is a fabulous bag for your body. It's stretchy and waterproof. It helps to control your body's temperature, and it protects you from germs.

In most places, your skin is about 1/16 in (2mm) thick.

A unique print
Everybody has a unique set of fingerprints, but there are three main types: arch, loop, and whorl.

Skin facts

● About 50,000 tiny flakes of dead skin drop off your body every minute!

● Millions of microscopic dust mites live in your bed, gobbling up the skin flakes that fall off you.

Sweat it off
You sweat to keep cool – but did you know that in a fingernail-sized patch of skin there are between 100 and 600 sweat glands?

Skin alert...cure that cut!
Cut yourself and a lot of activity in the surrounding skin causes the blood to clot. The resulting scab stops dirt and germs from getting in.

What's a bruise?
Bruises are caused by damage to the tiny blood capillaries that run just under the skin's surface. If broken by a heavy knock, they bleed into the surrounding area.

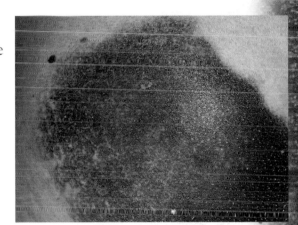

What's underneath?
Skin contains sweat glands, hair follicles, nerve endings, and tiny blood vessels called capillaries. Underneath, there's a layer of fat.

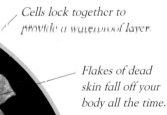

Cells lock together to provide a waterproof layer.

Flakes of dead skin fall off your body all the time.

My feet are wrinkly!
Spend a long time swimming and the thicker skin on your feet and hands will begin to wrinkle because water has soaked into it. The extra water makes it pucker up.

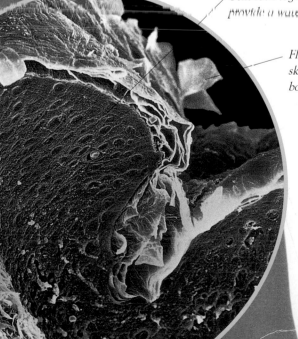

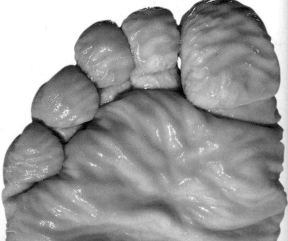

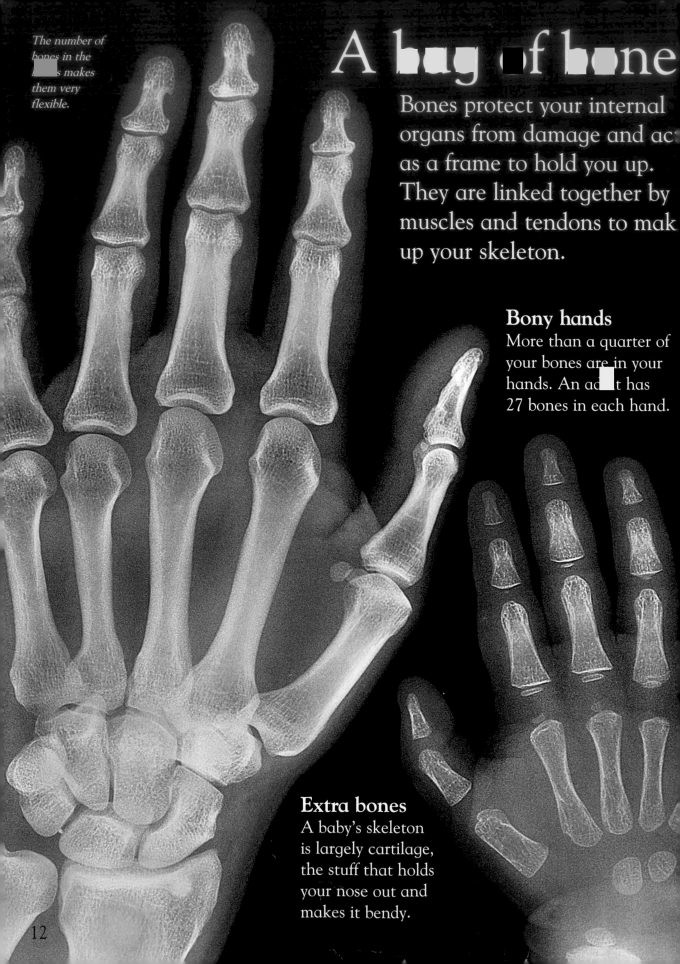

The number of bones in the
makes
them very
flexible.

A bag of bone

Bones protect your internal
organs from damage and ac
as a frame to hold you up.
They are linked together by
muscles and tendons to mak
up your skeleton.

Bony hands

More than a quarter of
your bones are in your
hands. An ad t has
27 bones in each hand.

Extra bones

A baby's skeleton
is largely cartilage,
the stuff that holds
your nose out and
makes it bendy.

s broken!

ou break a bone, an X-ray
ows the doctor what is going
 beneath the skin. Bones
 living tissue, and will
ually mend, with rest and
pport, in about 6–8 weeks.

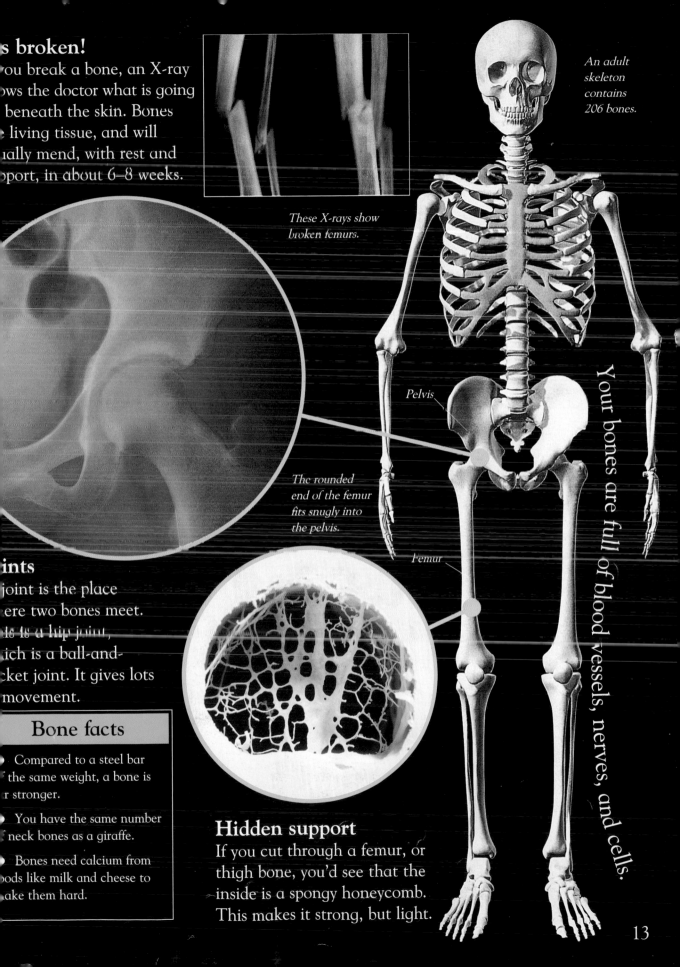

These X-rays show
broken femurs.

An adult
skeleton
contains
206 bones.

Pelvis

The rounded
end of the femur
fits snugly into
the pelvis.

Femur

Your bones are full of blood vessels, nerves, and cells.

ints

 joint is the place
ere two bones meet.
is is a hip joint,
ich is a ball-and-
cket joint. It gives lots
 movement.

Bone facts

 Compared to a steel bar
 the same weight, a bone is
r stronger.

 You have the same number
 neck bones as a giraffe.

 Bones need calcium from
ods like milk and cheese to
ake them hard.

Hidden support

If you cut through a femur, or
thigh bone, you'd see that the
inside is a spongy honeycomb.
This makes it strong, but light.

13

Hairy stuff

Your hair and nails are made of the same thing. It's called keratin, and most of it is dead. In fact, your hair and nails are only alive at the roots. That's why it doesn't hurt to cut your hair or trim your nails.

A hairy tale

Hair grows over most of your body. The thickest is on your head, where you have between 100,000 and 150,000 hairs!

This close-up of eyelash hairs shows how they grow from follicles in the skin.

Each hair is made of overlapping plates of keratin.

14

...ratchy head?

...our head itches,
...may have head
.... You can see
...ir eggs as tiny
...ite spots in the
...r above your ear.

Head lice

Head lice love
to cling to hair,
suck our blood,
and lay their
eggs. Get rid
of them with
special shampoo.

A female head louse
will lay 50–150 eggs.

Fingernails grow four times faster than toenails.

...e you right-handed?

...o, the nails on this hand
...l grow faster than those
...the left. This is controlled
...the brain.

Like hair, your nails
are made of millions
of overlapping
plates of keratin.

15

Move that bod

Step forward and you'll use about 200 muscles. You have at least 600 muscles, and they are responsib for every movement you make, from jumping to blinking to breathing.

A closer look

A muscle is made up of bundles of tiny fibers. Each fiber is incredibly thin – much thinner than a hair.

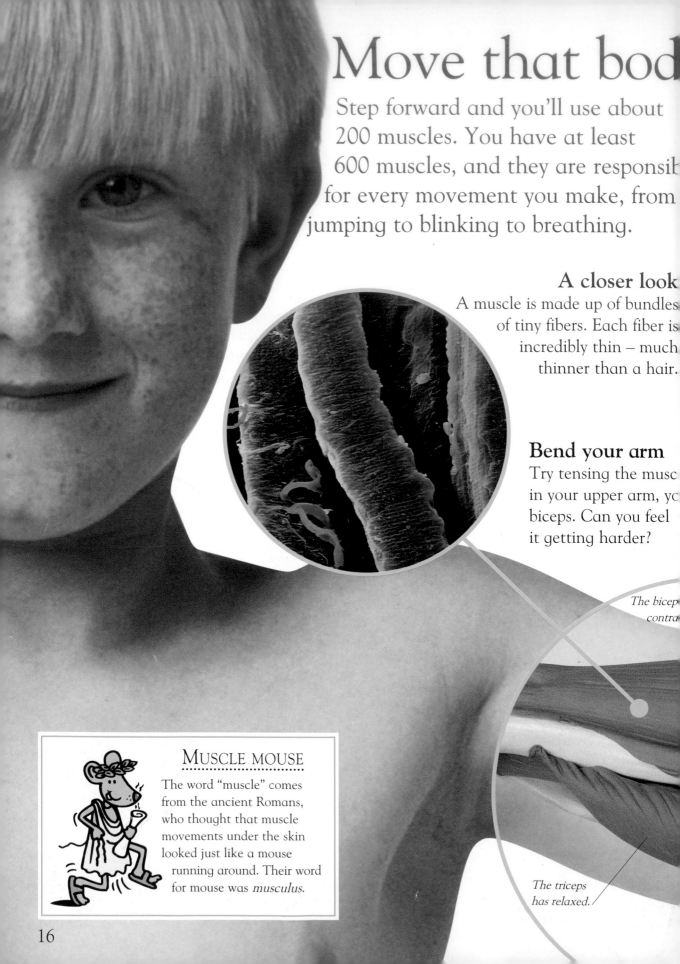

Bend your arm

Try tensing the musc in your upper arm, yo biceps. Can you feel it getting harder?

The bicep contra

The triceps has relaxed.

MUSCLE MOUSE

The word "muscle" comes from the ancient Romans, who thought that muscle movements under the skin looked just like a mouse running around. Their word for mouse was *musculus*.

l joined up

ny muscles are
ed to the ends
he bones they
trol by stringy
ds called tendons.

*Clench your fist and
you can see a tendon
working under the
skin of your wrist.*

Muscle facts

- Your muscles make up 40 percent of your body's weight.

- Help your muscles grow big and strong by eating lots of protein. That means lots of eggs, meat, cheese, and beans.

- Muscles can contract to one-third of their size.

Make a face!

Your face is full of muscles. Incredibly, you use 17 of these muscles to smile. However, you use about 40 muscles to frown!

w do they work?

scles can only pull, so they
rk in pairs. In your arm, the
eps pulls by contracting to
d the arm and the triceps
ls to straighten it.

*As a muscle contracts, it gets shorter and harder.
As a muscle relaxes, it gets longer and softer.*

*The muscles in
our face allow us
to make about 10,000
different facial expressions!*

Pump that blood!

Can you feel your heart beat? This amazing muscle never gets tired, even though it opens and closes about 100,000 times a day, every day, throughout your life.

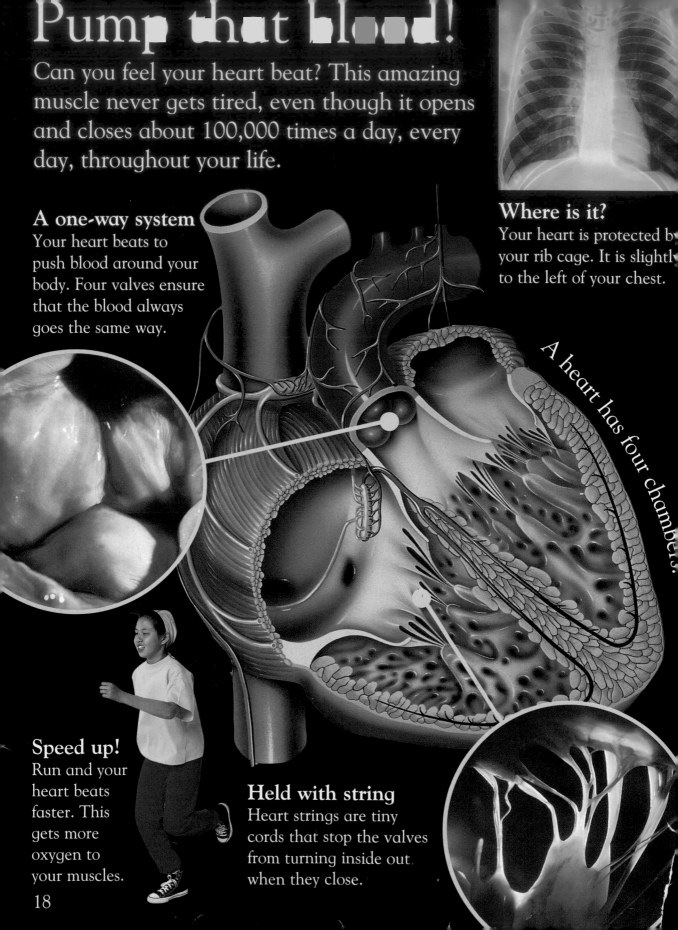

A one-way system

Your heart beats to push blood around your body. Four valves ensure that the blood always goes the same way.

Where is it?

Your heart is protected by your rib cage. It is slightly to the left of your chest.

A heart has four chambers.

Speed up!

Run and your heart beats faster. This gets more oxygen to your muscles.

Held with string

Heart strings are tiny cords that stop the valves from turning inside out when they close.

What is blood?

Blood is made up of a watery liquid called plasma, red cells, white cells, and fragments of cells called platelets.

Plasma makes up about 55 percent of your blood.

A tangled web

This is what happens when your blood clots because of a cut. The red cells are caught in a mesh of fibers. They die and stop blood from flowing out.

The mesh forms very rapidly.

Heart/blood facts

- At rest, a child's heart beats about 85 times a minute.

- A drop of blood contains approximately 250 million red cells, 275,000 white cells, and 16 million platelets.

- A blood cell goes around your body and back through your heart more than 1,000 times each day.

Red cells are doughnut-shaped.

Fighting infection

White blood cells and platelets make up less than one percent of blood. They fight germs.

Red blood cells

Red blood cells make up about 44 percent of your blood. Millions are made and destroyed every second.

A circular tale

Your heart pumps blood around your body through arteries and veins. Arteries carry blood away from the heart. Veins carry blood toward the heart.

Most to the brain
Your brain needs a constant supply of oxygen-rich blood. It is so important that it gets 20 percent of your body's blood supply.

Blood supply to the brain.

Your brain is the hottest part of your body.

Most veins (shown in blue) carry blood that contains carbon dioxide, a waste gas.

Brain

Lung

Lung

Stomach

Kidney

Liver

Kidney

Smaller and smaller
Arteries and veins become a branching network of capillaries. The capillary walls are so thin that gases, nutrients, and waste products pass easily through.

A change of color
As blood travels through the lungs, it picks up oxygen. This makes it brighter in color. As it releases oxygen around the body, it grows darker.

Most arteries (shown in red) carry blood rich with oxygen and food.

Your blood vessels stretch 99,400 miles (160,000 km).

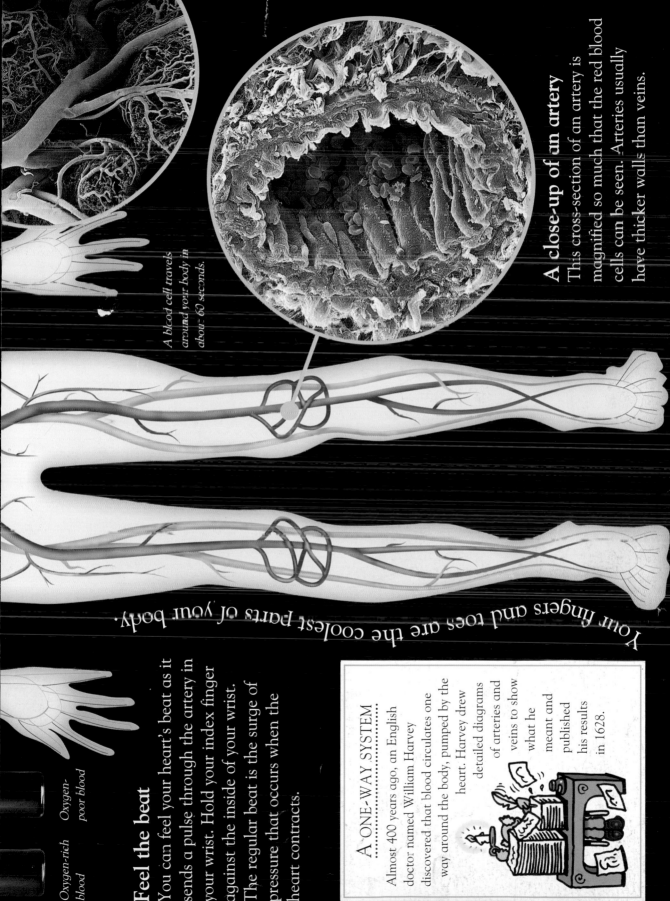

A close-up of an artery

This cross-section of an artery is magnified so much that the red blood cells can be seen. Arteries usually have thicker walls than veins.

A blood cell travels around your body in about 60 seconds.

Your fingers and toes are the coolest parts of your body.

Oxygen-rich blood

Oxygen-poor blood

Feel the beat

You can feel your heart's beat as it sends a pulse through the artery in your wrist. Hold your index finger against the inside of your wrist. The regular beat is the surge of pressure that occurs when the heart contracts.

A ONE-WAY SYSTEM

Almost 400 years ago, an English doctor named William Harvey discovered that blood circulates one way around the body, pumped by the heart. Harvey drew detailed diagrams of arteries and veins to show what he meant and published his results in 1628.

Puff, puff

Believe it or not, you take about 23,000 breaths each day. With every breath, you take in oxygen, which you need to stay alive, and you breathe out a gas called carbon dioxide, which your body doesn't need.

Air passes down your windpipe, or trachea, and into your two lungs.

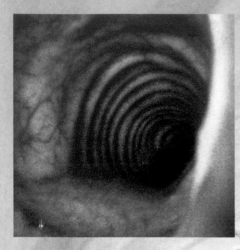

A wind tunnel

Air travels down your windpipe, or trachea, to get to your lungs. In this photograph, you can see the rings of cartilage that hold the trachea open.

Taking out the oxygen

The air tubes (shown red) get smaller and smaller until they end in millions of tiny air sacs called alveoli. Here, oxygen is taken into your blood.

Air tube

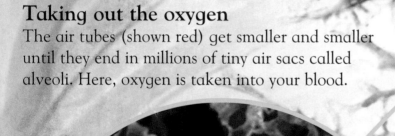

These spaces are air sacs called alveoli.

Lung facts

● Stethoscopes, which doctors use to check breathing, were invented in 1816.

● You breathe faster during and after exercise to draw more oxygen into your body.

● Your left lung is smaller than your right lung to allow room for your heart.

Blowing bubbles

We can only store oxygen for a short time in our lungs. Also, unlike fish, we have no gills to remove oxygen from water. So we cannot stay underwater without an air supply.

WHY DO I GET HICCUPS?

Hiccups happen when the muscle that helps to move air in and out of your lungs, your diaphragm, jerks uncontrollably. Nobody really knows why they happen, but there are lots of suggestions for stopping them. Try breathing into a paper bag...or ask a friend to scare you...or (yummy!) put sugar under your tongue.

There's water, too

Your breath contains water. If you breathe onto a cold surface, this water condenses into tiny droplets. That means it changes from a vapor into a liquid. The same thing happens on a cold day.

23

Attack of the bug

Everywhere you go, you are surrounded
by nasty germs, and many of them
want to live inside your body.
After all, it makes a comfy home.
The problem is, they can make you ill.

What are germs?

Germs fall into two
main groups: bacteria
and viruses. Your
body is good at
keeping them out,
but they are clever
at finding ways in.

Beastly bacteria

Bacteria come in lots of
funny shapes. Some even
have tails! If a cut becomes
infected (it will look red and
swollen), that's because
bacteria have gotten in.

Bacteria can double their numbers in 20 minutes!

Vile viruses

Have you had chicken pox?
It's caused by a virus. So is the
common cold. Viruses are tiny –
far smaller than bacteria.

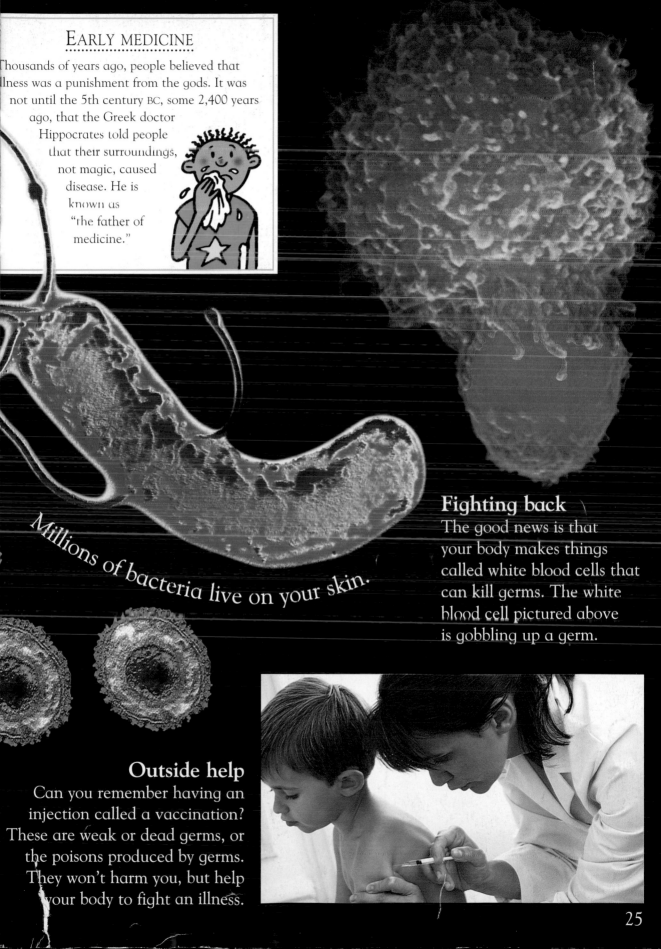

EARLY MEDICINE

Thousands of years ago, people believed that illness was a punishment from the gods. It was not until the 5th century BC, some 2,400 years ago, that the Greek doctor Hippocrates told people that their surroundings, not magic, caused disease. He is known as "the father of medicine."

Millions of bacteria live on your skin.

Fighting back

The good news is that your body makes things called white blood cells that can kill germs. The white blood cell pictured above is gobbling up a germ.

Outside help

Can you remember having an injection called a vaccination? These are weak or dead germs, or the poisons produced by germs. They won't harm you, but help your body to fight an illness.

hide

ug

giggle

Let's talk

There are many ways of "talking" and not all of them are with your lips. The look on your face and the way you stand tell people a about what you are thinking.

I need it now!

Babies can't talk, so they cry to let you know that they want something. From early on, they also communicate by eye contact and facial expression.

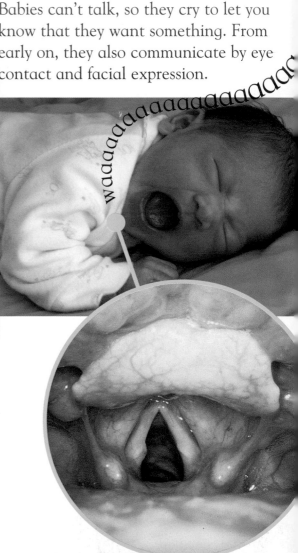

waaaaaaaaaaaaaaaaaac

Making a word

You make sounds as you breathe out over your voice box, or larynx. Your tongue, lip and teeth change the sounds into words.

hat do you think?

dy language can say a lot
out the way you feel. Throw
r arms in the air and
ople know you're excited.
e these children sad?

*It is thought
that at least
80 percent of
communication
is through body
language.*

shout

n language

alny is one way that people who are
f can communicate. They use their
ds to sign words and to spell letters.

*Some signed words
use one hand,
others use two.*

whisper

cry

27

Brainpower

Step forward, touch something, ta[lk]
drink a glass of milk…everythin[g]
you do is controlled by your
brain. It's a bit like a compute[r]
but far more complicated – a[nd]
it only weighs 2.9 lb (1.3 kg)!

Sight

Smell

Taste

Touch

Use those senses!
A simple drink requires a lot of bra[in]
power. Your eyes and fingers send
messages about what you see an[d]
touch, while your nose and
tongue help you to smell
and taste the contents.

*Nerves in this girl's
fingers "tell" her mu[scles]
to grip the glass.*

Brain facts

● The brain needs oxygen to
work properly. In fact, one-
fifth of all the oxygen you
breathe in goes to the brain.

● The brain is 85% water.

● The spinal cord stops
growing when you are about
five years old, having reached
about 17 in (43 cm).

How does it work?
Your brain contains billi[ons]
of nerve cells called
neurons that carry signa[ls]
to and from different par[ts]
of your body through you[r]
central nervous system.

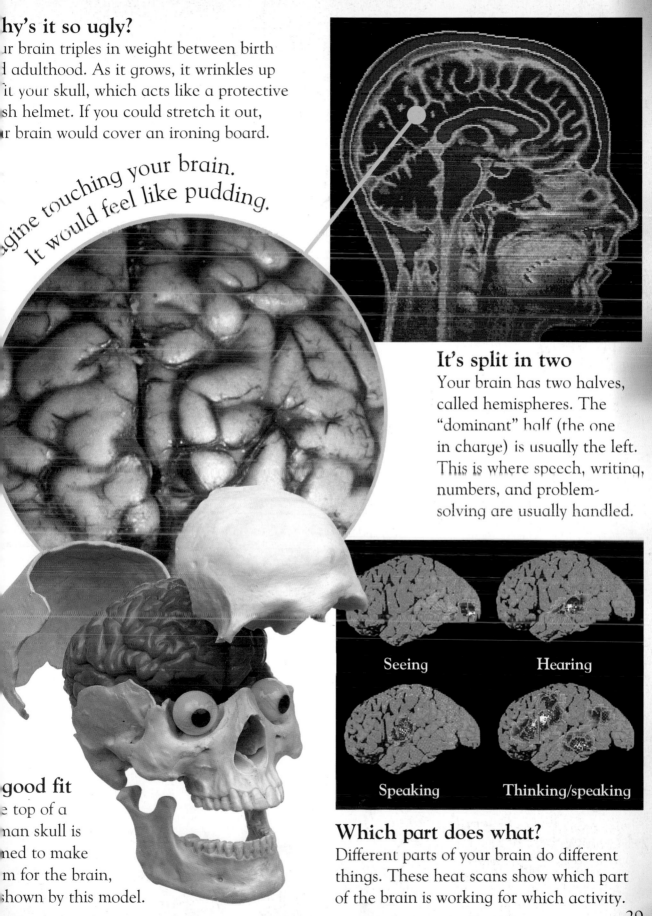

hy's it so ugly?
r brain triples in weight between birth
d adulthood. As it grows, it wrinkles up
it your skull, which acts like a protective
sh helmet. If you could stretch it out,
r brain would cover an ironing board.

*agine touching your brain.
It would feel like pudding.*

It's split in two
Your brain has two halves,
called hemispheres. The
"dominant" half (the one
in charge) is usually the left.
This is where speech, writing,
numbers, and problem-
solving are usually handled.

Seeing   Hearing

Speaking   Thinking/speaking

good fit
e top of a
nan skull is
ned to make
m for the brain,
shown by this model.

Which part does what?
Different parts of your brain do different
things. These heat scans show which part
of the brain is working for which activity.

smooth

slimy

Touch

When you touch
something, tiny touch
sensors in your skin
send a message to
your brain.

soft

wet *and* cold

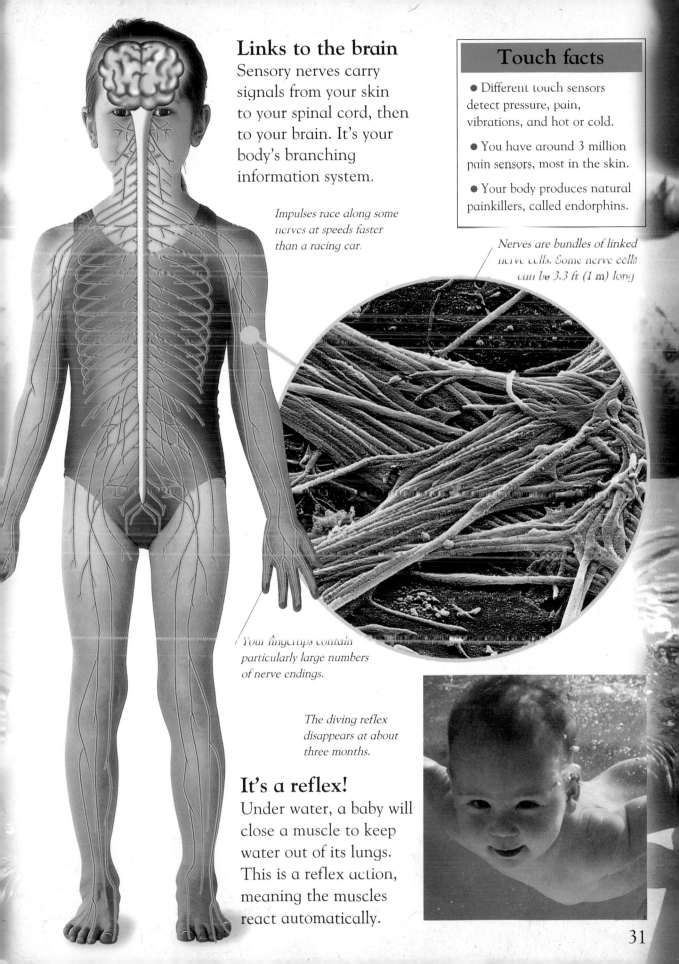

Links to the brain
Sensory nerves carry signals from your skin to your spinal cord, then to your brain. It's your body's branching information system.

Impulses race along some nerves at speeds faster than a racing car.

Touch facts
● Different touch sensors detect pressure, pain, vibrations, and hot or cold.

● You have around 3 million pain sensors, most in the skin.

● Your body produces natural painkillers, called endorphins.

Nerves are bundles of linked nerve cells. Some nerve cells can be 3.3 ft (1 m) long

Your fingertips contain particularly large numbers of nerve endings.

The diving reflex disappears at about three months.

It's a reflex!
Under water, a baby will close a muscle to keep water out of its lungs. This is a reflex action, meaning the muscles react automatically.

Listen up!

Your ear has three parts: the outer ear, which you can see; the middle ear, where there are tiny bones; and the inner ear, which contains a coiled tube of liquid.

A waxy tunnel

The small bits of dust and dirt that get into your ears are caught in your sticky ear wax. This gradually carries them out of your ear.

The eardrum separa the outer ear and middle e

There are 4,000 wax glands in each

People's ears never stop growing. In fact, they grow about ¼ in (6.35 mm) in 30 years.

Bones in your ear?

The bones in your middle ear – the malleus (hammer), incus (anvil), and stapes (stirrup) – are the smallest bones in your body.

Ma

...als travel to the ...n along ...e.

Tiny hairs are moved by sounds.

Hairs in your ear?

Tiny hairs in your inner ear pick up movements in the liquid around them. These are sent, as signals, to your brain to "hear."

These tiny hairs are found in the inner ear, in the cochlea. They link up to the brain.

Ear facts

● Human beings can tell the difference between more than 1,500 different tones of sound.

● Everybody's ears are shaped differently.

● The stapes is the smallest bone in your body; it's shorter than a grain of rice.

Why do I get dizzy?

Your ears tell your brain the position of your head. When you spin, your brain finds it difficult to keep up with the messages sent from your ears. So you feel dizzy.

A little help

If someone is deaf, it means that they cannot hear. A hearing aid helps partially deaf people to hear by making sounds louder.

Eye, eye

Those soft, squidgy balls in your head – your eyes – are well protected. They nestle in bony eye sockets and can hide behind your eyelids. Through them, your brain receives much of its information about the world.

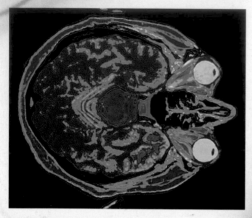

Take a peek inside

This picture shows the two eyes (yellow) in their eye sockets – separated by the nose. They connect directly to the brain.

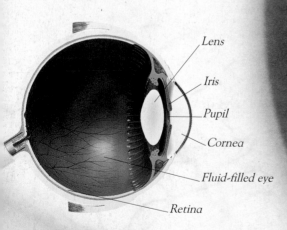

Lens

Iris

Pupil

Cornea

Fluid-filled eye

Retina

What's your color?

Blue, green, gray, or brown…what color are your eyes? The color of your iris depends on the instructions for eye color that you inherit from your parents.

Your eyes constantly water to keep them free of germs and dust.

A liquid camera

Your eyes are a bit like tiny video cameras, but filled with fluid. Light enters the eye through a hole in the iris, the pupil, and travels to the retina. Messages are sent to the brain, which tells you what you see.

The pupil is smaller in bright light.

The pupil is larger (to let in more light) in dim light.

Your eye can spy a lighted candle 1 mile (1.6 km) away!

How big are your pupils?

Pupil size changes depending on the light – and on what's around you. Do you like what you see? Your pupils will often get bigger. Bored? Your pupils will get smaller.

Eye facts

- You blink about 9,400 times a day.

- Six muscles hold each eye. They are kept busy, moving about 100,000 times a day!

- Microscopic eight-legged mites live in the base of your eyelashes. A yucky fact? Not really – they eat up nasty germs for you.

What is color blindness?

Your retina contains pigments that detect color. If these are not working, you will have difficulty telling some colors apart. This is known as color blindness.

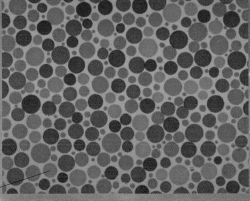

Can you see this number? If not, the pigment that picks up red light may be missing from your retina.

Smelly stuff

Did you know that humans have the ability to tell the difference between about 10,000 smells? This incredible sense helps you to taste and enjoy things.

How do we smell?

Things have a smell because they give off particles called molecules. Sniff something and these travel up to cilia at the top of your nose. Under the microscope, cilia look like tiny hairs.

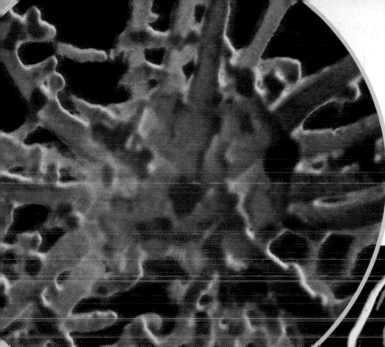

Smell receptors

When the molecules reach the top of your nose, they dissolve in the mucus (or snot) that your nose constantly produces. They then travel to the smell receptors.

Cells at the top of your nose produce about 2 pints (1 liter) of mucus a day.

You have 10 million smell receptors.

A path to the brain

The smell receptors then send a message to your brain, which either recognizes the smell or memorizes it if it hasn't come across it before.

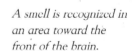

A smell is recognized in an area toward the front of the brain.

aaa aaaa atchooooooo

Why do flowers make me sneeze?

you have an allergic reaction to pollen, too much icus will pour into your nose to try to flush it out. ere's so much that you have to sneeze to get rid of it.

Smell facts

• A bloodhound's sense of smell is 1,000 times better than a human's.

• Mucus is a clear fluid. It mixes with things in the air, and they give it a color.

• The mucus in your nose can become green if you have an infection.

Fun with taste

Have you ever wondered what your tongue does? It helps you to talk, but it also helps you to move food around your mouth, and, more importantly, to taste it.

Take a sniff
Smell plays an important part when you taste a food. That's why things don't taste so good if you have a blocked nose.

Ten thousand taste buds help y... to tell the difference betwe... four different flavors.

If your frenulum is short, you will not be able to stick your tongue out very far.

Anchored in place
A flap of skin called the frenulum holds the bottom of your tongue to the floor of your mouth. It stops you from swallowing your tongue.

Tastes on your tongue

When food enters your mouth, pieces dissolve in saliva. Saliva makes food easier to swallow, but it also means the food flavor can be detected by taste buds. Different flavors are detected in different places.

Area where sour flavors are detected

The tip of your tongue can tell if something is sweet

Bitter flavors are picked up toward the back of your mouth

Area where salty tastes are picked up

Larger, flat-topped papillae contain taste buds.

Smaller papillae help the tongue to "grip" slippery food such as ice cream.

Why the bumps?

Your tongue is bumpy so things don't slip off easily. It is covered in round papillae, some of which contain taste buds.

Taste facts

● Each taste bud cell is renewed after about 7 days.

● Your tongue has touch sensors, to help you feel food.

● More than 1 quart (1 liter) of saliva is released into your mouth each day.

39

Take a bite

Before their first teeth appear, babies drink milk or eat puréed food. Without teeth, they cannot chew on food to make it easier to swallow. Teeth are very important.

The large knobbly teeth at the back are molars.

Incisor

Molar

A child has 20 milk teeth.

There are 32 adult teeth.

How big are they?

Each of your teeth has a long root, which holds it tightly in your jaw. Inside each tooth are nerves and blood vessels.

Canines are slightly pointed. They help to tear food.

Teeth are rooted in your gums.

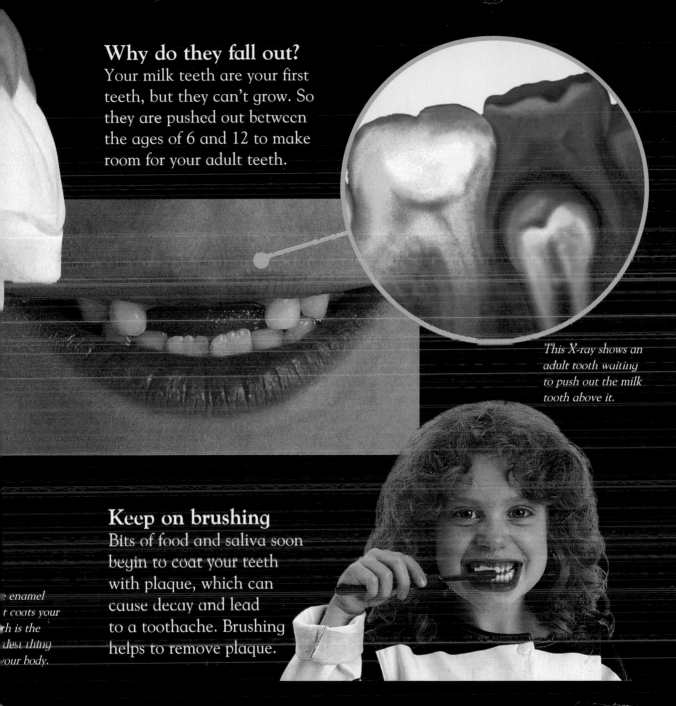

Why do they fall out?

Your milk teeth are your first teeth, but they can't grow. So they are pushed out between the ages of 6 and 12 to make room for your adult teeth.

This X-ray shows an adult tooth waiting to push out the milk tooth above it.

Keep on brushing

Bits of food and saliva soon begin to coat your teeth with plaque, which can cause decay and lead to a toothache. Brushing helps to remove plaque.

e enamel
t coats your
th is the
dest thing
our body.

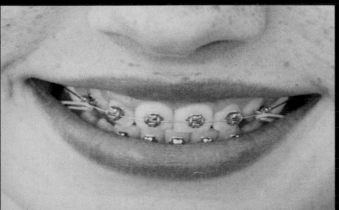

Why do I need braces?

Sometimes your teeth grow crookedly. Braces help to straighten them, making them sit evenly in your mouth.

The braces put a gentle pressure on each tooth.

From food to poo

Food gives us many things, including the energy to run and jump. Energy is also used to break down or digest the food we eat. The nutrients this releases are passed to our cells through the bloodstream. Cells use nutrients to make more energy.

An acid bath
Acid is released in your stomach to break down the food. A constant churning helps turn the food into a mushy soup.

Food travels from your mouth to your stomach in the time it takes you to read this sentence – about ten seconds.

Going down
After you have chewed your food, it is pushed down a tube called the esophagus and into your stomach.

The sphincter muscle lets food out of your stomach.

You munch your way through some 1,100 lb (500 kg) of food each year. That's the weight of a small car.

Taking the nutrients
The small intestine is lined with fingerlike villi. Blood runs through the villi, where it can pick up goodies from the food and take them to the liver. The liver removes

Don't lose the water!
The remains of your food spend up to two days in the large intestines, which absorb water from it. Strong muscles push it along.

half of poo is made up of bacteria

Muscle action pushes the broken-down food matter along the intestines.

The broken-down food spends up to 3 hours in the small intestine.

Waiting to go
The rectum is where your feces, or poo, are stored, waiting for you to use the bathroom. This is waste that your body is unable to use.

Stomach facts
• Acid in your stomach could dissolve an iron nail.
• Your stomach can hold about 15 cups of water.
• A thick layer of mucus protects the stomach from its own acid.

Sleep tight

After all the activities you do each day, your body needs to rest. Sleep gives your brain a chance to catch up with what you've done. Without it, you cannot think properly and your body will begin to slow down.

Why do I yawn?

If you are bored or sleepy, your breathing slows. You yawn to pull more oxygen in your body, helping to keep you awake.

Miss a night's sleep and you'll be crabby and clumsy the next day.

A five-year-old needs about ten hours of sleep each night.

You wriggle around a lot when you're sleeping, changing position about 45 times a night.

WHERE ARE YOU GOING?

Sometimes people walk in their sleep. They may even get dressed, or try to find something to eat. But when they wake up in the morning, they won't remember anything about it. More children sleepwalk than adults, and more boys than girls. Nobody really knows why people sleepwalk, but it is usually harmless.

What was that?

Children sometimes have frightening dreams called nightmares, usually about being chased. Remember, nightmares are not real.

Sleep facts

● We spend about one-third of our lives asleep.

● Most people have about 4–5 dreams every night – but you won't remember them all.

● A dream lasts between 5 and 30 minutes.

It can be noisy!

Snoring happens if a person cannot move air easily through the nose and mouth during sleep. It causes a loud noise.

ZZZZZZ

A growth hormone is released when a child is asleep.

Why do I dream?

Dreams bring pictures of things you have seen during the day, but also images that are unrelated to the day's events. Nobody knows exactly why people dream.

zzzzzzZZZZZZZZZZZZZZzz

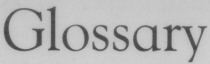

Glossary

Here are the meanings of some words it is useful to know when learning about the human body.

Alveoli microscopic airbags inside the lungs. These are where oxygen from air breathed in is passed into the blood.

Artery part of the network of vessels that carry blood around the body. Arteries carry blood away from the heart.

Blood vessel one of the arteries, veins, and capillaries that carry blood through the body.

Carbon dioxide the waste gas that humans breathe out.

Cartilage tough but flexible material that makes up much of a baby's skeleton. Smaller amounts are found in an adult's body.

Cell one of the body's basic building blocks.

Central nervous system the part of the body's communication system that consists of the brain and the spinal cord.

Diaphragm the muscle that stretches across the chest just below the lungs and helps a person to breathe.

Digestion the process of breaking down food.

Esophagus the tube that runs between the throat and the stomach.

Feces the solid waste that is produced by digestion.

Germs the microscopic bacteria and viruses that cause sickness.

Intestines the long tubes through which food passes in the process of digestion.

Larynx the part of the throat where speech sounds are made.

Mucus a slippery fluid that is found in areas such as the respiratory and digestive system.

Muscle a tissue that contracts to cause movement.

Nerve a bundle of fibers through which instructions pass between different areas and cells in the body.

Nutrients the substances in food that are useful to the body (such as proteins, carbohydrates, and vitamins).

Organ one of a number of different parts of the body that each perform a particular job.

Oxygen the gas that humans take from air. Oxygen is needed to release energy from food.

Plasma the part of blood that remains when the red and white cells are removed.

Pore tiny holes in the skin through which the body sweats.

Reflex an automatic action, such as breathing or blinking.

Saliva a fluid released into the mouth that helps begin the breakdown of food and makes it slippery enough to swallow.

ses the means by which
nans find out about the world
und them. The five senses
: hearing, sight, taste, touch,
d smell.

nal cord the bundle of nerves
t runs inside the backbone.

eat a liquid that contains waste
ducts. It is released through
es in the skin to help the body
l down.

adon a tough cord that links
scle to bone.

chea the tube that runs
m the larynx to the lungs.

abilical cord the cord that
nects a fetus to its mother
ough the placenta.

ccination an injection of
d or weak germs, or the
ins produced by germs, that
ches the body to fight that
ticular germ.

in part of the network of
sels that carry blood around
body. Veins carry blood
ard the heart.

rtebra one of the bones that
ke up the backbone.

li Fingerlike projections from
wall of the small intestines
ough which nutrients are
en into the blood.

ice box see larynx.

Index

Acknowledgments

Dorling Kindersley would like to thank: Dorian Spencer Davies and Andrew O'Brien for original artwork, and Sonia Whillock for design assistance.

Picture credits

The publisher would like to thank the following for their kind permission to reproduce their photographs:
(Key: a=above; c=center; b=below; l=left; r=right; t=top)

Corbis: 14tl, 26cr, 27tr, 31br, 35br, 38l. **Foodpix:** 28. **Getty Images:** 2-3, 4tr, 5tr, 26bl, 27br, 30bl, 33bl, 36, 44-5, 46-7, 48. **ImageState:** 1, 11br, 17cr, 23tr, 27cla, 30tl, 30tr, 30br, 39tr. **Age Fotostock** 4-5b. **Imagingbody.com:** 13cb, 15br. **Masterfile UK:** 41bl. **Allen**

Birnbach 26tl. **Robert Karpa** 45tl. **Gail Mooney** 26cl. **Brian Pi** 27cr. **Science Photo Library:** 6-7t, 7cl, 7br, 8tr, 8ca, 8bl, 8br, 9, 10-11t, 11tr, 11cr, 11bl, 12, 13tc, 13cl, 13r, 14bl, 14br, 15tc, 15cl, 15bl, 16c, 17tl, 18tr, 18cl, 18br, 18, 19tc, 19c, 21tc, 22tl, 22tc, 22c 22bl, 22-23, 24tl, 24bl, 24-25b, 24-25t, 25tr, 25br, 26br, 31cr, 33tl 5, 35tc, 35tr, 36cr, 37tl, 37cr, 37bl, 42tl, 42-4 t, 43bl. **BSIP/VEM** 40tr. **Gregory Dimijian** 34cla. **Pascal Goetgheluck** 40. **Mehau Kulyk** 29tr. **Omikron** 39c. **Geoff Tompkinson** 29cl. **Wellcome Dept. of Cognitive Neurology** 29br. **The Wellcome Institute Library, London:** 32cr.

Jacket images: Front cover – Corbis Stock Market: (t). Getty Images: (br). Science Photo Library: (bc, c). **Back cover** – Scie Photo Library. All other images – © Dorling Kindersley. For further information, see www.dkimages.com